Mathematics

Book 5

- *Large Numbers & Basic Operations*
- *Simplification of Numerical Expressions*
- *Angles & Triangles*
- *Percentage*
- *Temperature*
- *Data Handling*
- *Multiples, Factors, Prime and Composite Numbers*

Seema Chawla, M.A., B.Ed.

1. Large Numbers (upto 10 Million) and Basic Operations

Let's recapitulate

The number system in Mathematics is infinite i.e. it can be extended to any number of digits. Now, we shall extend to 8 - digit numbers in class V. The value of a digit in a particular number is known as its **place value**.

These numbers can be represented as follows. Now put them in the place value chart given below:

79,865

1,534,986

10,000,000

9,340,628

83,625,354

Periods	Millions			Thousands			Ones		
PLACES	H. MILLION	TEN MILLION	MILLION	HUNDREDTH	TENTH	TH	H	T	O
1,534,986			1	5	3	4	9	8	6
10,000,000		1	0	0	0	0	0	0	0
9,340,628			9	3	4	0	6	2	8
83,625,354		8	3	6	2	5	3	5	4

We put commas between every two periods which help us in reading and writing the large numbers.

Read all the numbers in the chart aloud.

Come, Let's Play with Numbers

1. **Put commas in the following numbers according to International number system and write them in words:**

   a. 50869724 = _50,_____

   b. 7358864 = _____

   c. 4065937 = _____

   d. 25986409 = _____

2. **Fill in the missing numbers to complete the rows.**

   a. 25635924, 25735924, _____, _____, 26035924

   b. 1799843, 1789843, _____, _____, _____

3. **Write the following in numerals.**

   a. Eighty four million seven hundred thirty thousand four hundred fifty.

   (84,730,450)

   b. Nine million four hundred twenty five thousand sixty seven.

   (9,425,067)

4. **Understand & write.** (56897421)

   In the number given in the box, digit 8 stands at _____ place and the value of the digit is _800000_. The digit _____ is in the hundred thousands place and its value is _____.

How can Before and After numbers be found?

After number is +1 and is called the Successor.

Before number is −1 and is called the Predecessor.

1. **Give the Successor of:-**

   a. 3,258,657 → _____

   b. 41,398,256 → _____

2. **Give the Predecessor of:-**

   a. _____ ← 23,897,000

   b. _____ ← 465,425

3. **Now let's compare our numbers, whose number is greater?**

   Put the sign >, < or = to decide.

   My numbers are :   These are my numbers :

   a. 3487956   ◯   3497956

   b. 205867   ◯   905867

   c. 51389428   ◯   59389420

   d. 895779   ◯   859779

Roman Numbers & the Hindu Arabic Systems

Always remember these Roman symbols.

I	– 1
V	– 5
X	– 10
L	– 50
C	– 100
D	– 500
M	– 1000

1. **Now try combining the Roman Numbers to make these:-**

   a. 89   LXXXIX
   b. 98   _____
   c. 64   _____
   d. 26   _____
   e. 47   _____
   f. 100 _____
   g. 35   _____
   h. 152 _____
   i. 107 _____
   i. 125 _____

2. **Write the following Roman Expression in the Hindu Arabic System.**

   a. XC   _____
   b. LXIX   _____
   c. LXXX   _____
   d. XXC   _____
   e. D   _____
   f. XXXIV _____
   g. XXVI   _____
   h. CV   _____
   i. CXXIII _____
   j. XLIII _____

Try this:-

There are

_____ 5-digit numbers.
_____ 6-digit numbers.
_____ 7-digit numbers.
_____ 8-digit numbers.

Rounding off Numbers

Can you guess the number of marbles in this pitcher?

Yes. I have collected about 300 marbles. Tell me the exact number of marbles in the pitcher.

There are exactly 293 marbles in this pitcher 293 has been rounded off to 300.

How we round off numbers?

Tip:-
When rounding off tens place, consider ones place; for hundreds place consider tens place, for thousands place consider hundreds place and so on also with very large nos.

To the nearest ten (10)

Amanda has 23 sweets

Round off the number to the nearest tens

Amanda has around 20 sweets

We consider the digit which is one place before the digit to be rounded off.

> If the digit is < 5 we take the earlier tens and if it is more than t we take the next tens.

Round off to the nearest ten

31 _____ 353 _____ 1099 _____ 2685 _____

Round off to the nearest hundreds

142 _____ 4387 _____ 950 _____ 867 _____

Round off to the nearest thousands

8039 _____ 2736 _____ 1543 _____ 995 _____

Round off to the nearest hundred thousands

8430000 _____ 9563962 _____

235132 _____ 987950 _____

Try this:-

Smallest 3-digit no. _____

Greatest 4-digit no. _____

1 less than smallest 2-digit no. _____

1 more than greatest 5-digit no. _____

My Number Trick
- Choose a 3-digit number with 1st digit greater than the 3rd one.
- Reverse these digits
- Subtract
- Reverse the digits again
- Add
- See the answer

Try these numbers 451, 382, 734

Surprise ! Each time the answer will be 1089

```
    6 8 3
  - 3 8 6
    2 9 7
  + 7 9 2
  1 0 8 9
```

Find the product:-

a. 4 9 0 8 7
   ×   3 2 6

b. 1 1 3 2 1
   ×   7 0 4

c. 3 5 9 5 6 1
   ×   4 7

d. 2 5 0 7 9
   ×   1 5 0

Division:

Do you know how to divide?
Try this:-

1. Divide and write the quotient and remainder

a. 55) 3 7 4 9 4 9

b. 17) 4 0 7 8 6 3

Q =
R =

Q =
R =

2. **If a factory produces 376775 loaves of bread in a day, how many loaves will it produce in a year of 325 working days?**

   _____
   _____
   _____

   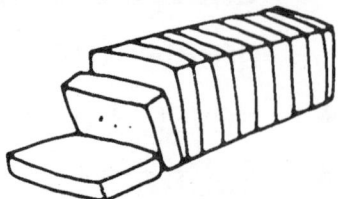

3. **Jack's yearly salary is $ 378450. How much does he earn in a month?**

   _____
   _____
   _____

4. **Quickly test your numbers.**

   a. 3495 + 6078 + _____ = 2915 + _____ + 3495

   b. 3072 – _____ = 30752

   c. _____ x 1 = 8465

   d. _____ ÷ 483 = 0

   e. 384 x 6000 = _____

   f. 30 x _____ = 30,000

   g. 295 x _____ = 2,95,000

   h. 100 x 1000 = _____

   i. 50750 ÷ _____ = 5075

   j. 150892 x 100 = _____

   k. 6357928 – _____ = 3891003

   l. 40007 – 29885 = _____

   m. 564320 + _____ = 798432

   n. 10000 + 10000 = _____

   o. 50000 – _____ = 49999

2. Multiples, Factors, Prime & Composite Numbers

Multiples

Let's Recapitulate:-

- For getting the multiples of a Number we have to recite the multiplication tables of these numbers.
- Every number is a multiple of 1 and itself.
- Even numbers are the multiples of 2 and odd numbers are those which are not the multiples of 2.
- There is no end to the multiples you can get for a particular no.

Let's Understand:-

a. Multiples of 4 will be
   4, 8, 12, 16 __ __ __ __

b. Multiples of 5 will be
   5, 10, 15, 20 __ __ __ __

c. Encircle the multiples of 7
   17   (21)   24   35   28   30   41   42

d. Encircle the multiples of 6
   11   16   12   35   30   48   49

e. First multiple of 10: ☐

   Third multiple of 5: ☐

   Sixth multiple of 7: ☐

Do it:- Read, understand and reply

A. Multiples of 2:- 2, 4,(6,)8, 10,(12) 14, 16,(18,)20, 22,(24) 26, 28,(30) 32, 34,(36) 38
   Multiples of 3:- 3,(6,)9,(12) 15,(18) 21,(24) 27,(30) 33,(36) 39

Common multiples of 2 and 3 are 6, 12, 18, 24, 30, 36 ....

Upper curves multiples of 2

Lower curves multiple of 3

6   12   18

Question:-

Write the five numbers which are common multiples of 2 and 3

6 , ☐ , ☐ , ☐ , ☐

B. Upper curves multiple of 4

Lower curves multiple of 6

Question:-

Write the 3 common multiples of 4 and 6

☐ , ☐ , ☐

Two common multiples of 4 and 6 are

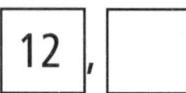
12 , ☐

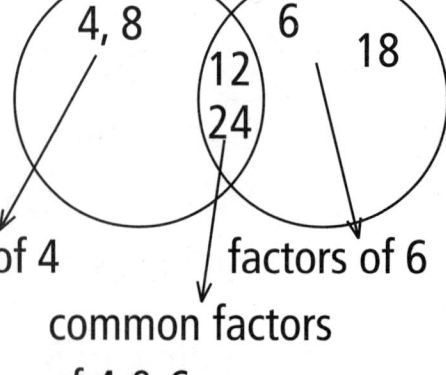
factors of 4   factors of 6
common factors of 4 & 6

Complete the blanks:-

1. Write the multiples of 2.

   = 2, 4, 6, ☐, 10, 12, ☐, 16, 18, 20, ☐, 24

2. Write the multiples of 3.
   = 3, ☐, 9, ☐, 15, ☐, ☐, ☐, 27, 30, ☐, 36.

3. Write the multiples of 8.
   = 8, 16, ☐, ☐, 40, ☐, ☐, ☐, 72, ☐, 88, ☐.

4. Write the 9th multiple of 9.
   = ☐.

5. Write all multiples of 10 between 85 and 125.
   = ☐, ☐, ☐, ☐.

6. Write the smallest six digit number.
   = ☐.

> 45...54
> Magic Numbers
> or
> Magic Multiples:-
> 45 = 9 x 5 = 45
> 45 number is multiple of number 9
> 45 ÷ 9 = 5
> Reverse of 45 is 54. Additon of digits 45 and 54
> (4 + 5) = 9
> (5 + 4) = 9
> 54 = 54 ÷ 9 = 6
> 6 x 9 = 54 so, 54 is also a multiple of 9

18 is a multiple of _____ and _____.

_____ is a multiple of 2 and 3.

105 is a multiple of _____, _____ and _____.

20 is a multiple of 4 and _____.

Factors: 1 is a factor of every number and also the smallest factor of any number.

- Every number is a factor of itself.
- Factor of a number is less than or equal to the number. Every number has atleast 2 factors: 1 & the number itself.
- When a number is divided by any of its factors it is divisible completely, there is no remainder.
- For example 24

    The multiplication facts of 24 are

    4 x 6, 6 x 4 = 24

    3 x 8, 8 x 3 = 24

    2 x 12, 12 x 2 = 24

    1 x 24, 24 x 1 = 24

So the factors of 24 are 1, 2, 3, 4, 6, 8, 12 and 24

Give the factors of 50, 60, 72, 96 showing their multiplication facts along.

Common factors of two numbers:-

Example: **8, 12**

Factors of 8:- 1, 2, 4, 8

factors of 12:- 1, 2, 3, 4, 6, 12

Common factors of 8 & 12 are 1, 2 and 4

Common factors of 10 and 5 are _____

Common factors of 5, 10 & 25 are _____

Common factors of 9, 24 and 27 are _____

Prime & Composite Numbers

No. which has exactly two factors 1 and the no. itself is a Prime Number 2, 3, 5, 7, 11, 13, 17 _ _ _ _ _ _ _ _ are Prime numbers.

1 is neither prime nor composite.

2 is the smallest prime number.

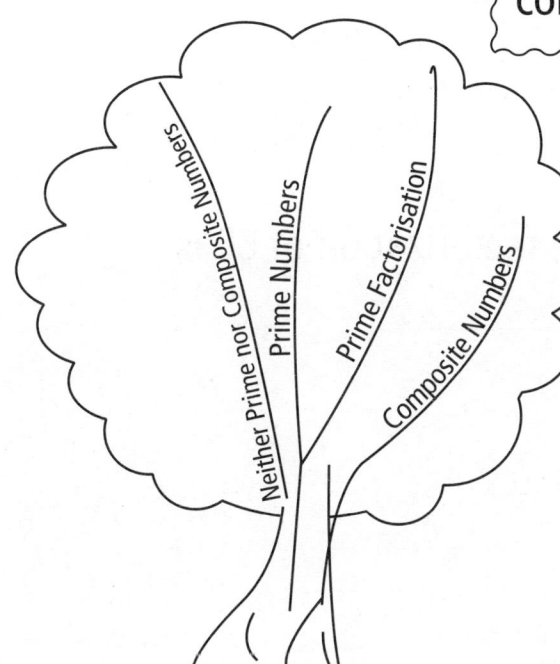

A no. which has more than two factors is called a composite numbers 4, 6, 8, 12, 24 are composite numbers.

4 is the smallest composite number.

The factorisation in which every factor is prime is called the Prime Factorization of the number. It will contain no composite number.

Do it yourself:-

✓ Tick the correct and ✗ the wrong statement.

a. 1 is the smallest prime number = ☐

b. 2 is a prime number = ☐

c. 97 is the greatest prime number less than 100 = ☐

d. Every prime number except 2 is odd = ☐

e. 12 has only two factors 1 and 12 = ☐

f. All even numbers are composite = ☐

Prime Factorization Method

Fill in the blanks

1.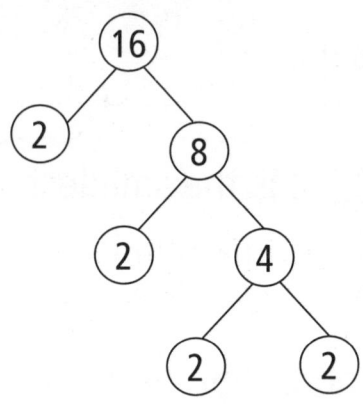

2.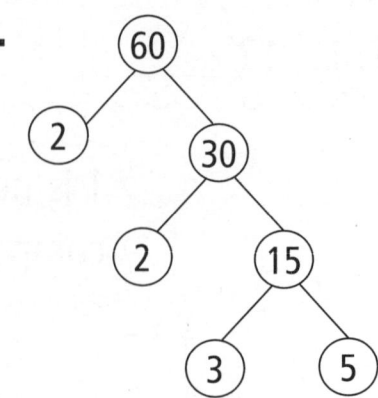

Prime factorization of 16 is
_____

Prime factorization of 60 is
_____

3. **Write the Smallest Number.**

   Prime number   _____
   Composite number   _____
   Odd Prime   _____
   Even composite   _____
   Odd composite   _____

4. **Encircle the Prime Numbers.**

   10, 17, 21, 25, 19, 37, 33, 45

5. **Encircle the Composite Numbers.**

   14, 15, 20 24, 27, 19, 17, 30, 32

6. **Fill in the blanks**

   a. Least multiple of 65 is _____
   b. Fourth multiple of 9 is _____
   c. Is 48 a multiple of 6? _____ (Yes/No)
   d. Is 7 a factor of 82 _____ (Yes/No)

e. 42 is a multiple of 7 (Yes/No)

f. Odd multiples of 3
   _____, _____, _____, _____

g. Even numbers between 20 and 35
   _____

h. 217 is divisible by 27 _____ (Yes/No)

7. Complete the following charts of H.C.F and L.C.M. A few have been done for you.

HCF	6	12	15	18	24	30	36
3	3						
6							
9				9			
12							
24						6	

LCM	2	4	6	8
2	2			
4				12
6				
8	8			
10				

Fill in the following boxes:-

Numbers 9 and 15

HCF = _____

LCM = _____

HCF | 3
15 × 9 = 135
LCM | 45
= 135

Numbers 12 and 18

HCF = _____

LCM = _____

HCF | ☐
12 × 18 = ☐
LCM | ☐
= ☐

3. Fractions

A fraction shows part of a whole. A whole can be a region or a collection. Rosy ordered 2 pizzas on her birthday.

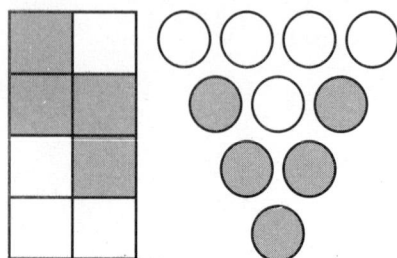

Equivalent fractions
$\frac{1}{2}, \frac{2}{4}, \frac{4}{8}, \frac{8}{16}$

Improper fractions
$\frac{3}{2}, \frac{10}{7}, \frac{9}{8}, \frac{13}{11}$
Denominator < Numerator

Proper fractions
$\frac{4}{7}, \frac{1}{5}, \frac{3}{11}, \frac{7}{11}$
Numerator < Denominator

Like fractions
$\frac{3}{7}, \frac{1}{7}, \frac{2}{7}, \frac{11}{7}, \frac{9}{7}$
Denominator is the same

Types of fractions

Unit fractions
$\frac{1}{2}, \frac{1}{7}, \frac{8}{16}, \frac{1}{17}$
Numerator is 1

Mixed No.
$3\frac{1}{10}, 2\frac{1}{13}, 3\frac{2}{4}, 8\frac{1}{3}$
Combination of whole and proper fraction

Unlike fractions
$\frac{1}{2}, \frac{2}{5}, \frac{4}{13}, \frac{8}{7}$
Denominator is different

 She divided one pizza into 2 equal parts and gave $\frac{1}{2}$ to her daughter.

 She divided the second pizza into 4 equal parts and gave $\frac{2}{4}$ to her son.

$\frac{1}{2} = \frac{2}{4}$ both get the same quantity. Isn't it amazing !

16

Let's understand fractions thoroughly:-

1. Compare the following fractions using >, < or =.

a. $\dfrac{6}{13} \bigcirc \dfrac{7}{13}$ b. $\dfrac{8}{11} \bigcirc \dfrac{2}{11}$ c. $\dfrac{4}{8} \bigcirc \dfrac{8}{16}$

2. Colour to show the fraction given below:-

a. $\dfrac{5}{8}$ b. $\dfrac{3}{4}$ c. $\dfrac{7}{10}$

3. a. Change into mixed fractions

$\dfrac{13}{5} = \square$

$\dfrac{19}{7} = \square$

$\dfrac{26}{13} = \square$

b. Change into improper fractions.

$2\dfrac{3}{5} = \square$

$1\dfrac{7}{9} = \square$

$4\dfrac{5}{7} = \square$

4. Rearrange the following fractions.

a. in ascending order $\dfrac{7}{8}, \dfrac{1}{6}, \dfrac{3}{4}, \dfrac{2}{3}$ | $\dfrac{11}{17}, \dfrac{9}{17}, \dfrac{12}{17}, \dfrac{2}{17}, \dfrac{8}{17}$

b. in descending order $\dfrac{2}{3}, \dfrac{1}{5}, \dfrac{1}{2}, \dfrac{5}{6}$ | $\dfrac{3}{15}, \dfrac{12}{15}, \dfrac{8}{15}, \dfrac{6}{15}, \dfrac{2}{15}$

5. Reduce the given fractions in the lowest terms:-

a. $\dfrac{18}{54}$ 	 b. $\dfrac{32}{48}$ 	 c. $\dfrac{24}{72}$

6. Give two equivalent fractions for each of these:-

a. $\dfrac{7}{9}$, _____, _____ 	 b. $\dfrac{6}{11}$, _____, _____

7. Solve these:-

a. $\dfrac{3}{13} \div \dfrac{9}{13}$ = _____

b. $16 \div \dfrac{4}{3}$ = _____

c. $\dfrac{5}{7} \times \dfrac{14}{25}$ = _____

d. $\dfrac{2}{15} \times \dfrac{45}{6}$ = _____

e. $\dfrac{4}{6} + \dfrac{8}{9} + \dfrac{2}{3}$ = _____

f. $\dfrac{7}{9} - \dfrac{7}{12}$ = _____

g. $3\dfrac{2}{5} - 2\dfrac{1}{10}$ = _____

h. Find the value of:-

$2\dfrac{3}{5} + 3\dfrac{1}{2} - 2\dfrac{1}{8}$ _____

Word Problems

1. Emily spent $\dfrac{1}{5}$ of her pocket money on ice cream and $\dfrac{1}{3}$ of it on story books. How much pocket money did she spend altogether?

_____

_____

2. David had $16\frac{2}{3}$ litres of petrol in his bike. He went for a ride, by the time he reached home he had only $2\frac{1}{3}$ litres left in the tank. How much petrol was used?

_____

_____

3. Daniel had a $\frac{3}{4}$ metre long rope. He wanted to cut it into 3 equal parts. What will be the length of each part of the rope?

_____

_____

4. If it takes $\frac{1}{2}$ minute to bake one bread, how many bread can be baked in $\frac{1}{4}$ hour?

_____

_____

5. Fill in the blanks.

a. $\frac{3}{6} \times \boxed{} = 0$

b. $\frac{1}{2} \times \frac{2}{3} \times \boxed{} = \frac{3}{5} \times \frac{2}{3} \times \boxed{}$

c. $1\frac{1}{3} \times \boxed{} = 1\frac{1}{3}$

d. $\frac{3}{6} \times 1 = \boxed{}$

e. $\frac{13}{17} \times 0 = \boxed{}$

f. $\frac{2}{5} \div \boxed{} = 1$

g. $\frac{2}{11}$ is the _____ of $\frac{11}{2}$

h. The reciprocal of $\frac{2}{5}$ is _____.

i. The reciprocal of 1 is always _____.

j. When we multiply reciprocals the product is _____.

k. _____ is the opposite of multiplication and vice versa.

l. a fraction divided by _____ is one

m. Zero divided by any fraction is _____.

4. Decimals

The word decimal comes from the latin word "decimus" meaning tenth decimal and is another way to write fractions whose denominators are 10, 100, 1000.

Decimals are often used in place of fractions to represent fractional numbers which are considered for more convenience in many ways. The place value of a digit becomes one tenth as the digit moves from left to right by one place. Decimals take less space in writing. It is easier to compare two fractional numbers using decimals.

Whole no. part (24).(67) Decimal part

read as twenty four point six seven

Zero divided by any decimal no. is zero.

Example:- in 2386 - place value of 6 = 6 x 1 = 6

in 2368 - place value of 6 is 6 x 10 = 60

so, the place value will be 6 ÷ 10 which is the same as $\frac{6}{10}$ we read $\frac{6}{10}$ as six - tenth.

Hundred	Tens	Ones	Tenths
100	10	1	$\frac{1}{10}$
		6		← 6 ones
			6	← 6 Tenths

Fractions are used to represent numbers smaller than 1. We can use decimals also to represent such fractional numbers.

Example:-

	Number	Fraction	Decimal
a.		$\frac{1}{10}$	0.1
b.		$\frac{2}{10}$	0.2
c.		$\frac{3}{10}$	0.3
d.		$\frac{4}{10}$	0.4

Note:- When we add or subtract we must write numbers correctly on both sides of the decimal

Add $ 50.50, $ 1.50, $ 300.25

```
              $    .   ¢
             50   .  50
              1   .  05
         +  300   .  25
Answer:-    351   .  80
```

Answer:- $ 351.80

Do it yourself (write as a decimal)

a. $\frac{8}{10}$ = ☐

b. $\frac{9}{100}$ = ☐

c. $\frac{68}{100}$ = ☐

d. $\frac{76}{1000}$ = ☐

Write as a fraction

a. 0.42 = _____

b. 0.30 = _____

c. 72.361 = _____

d. 10.037 = _____

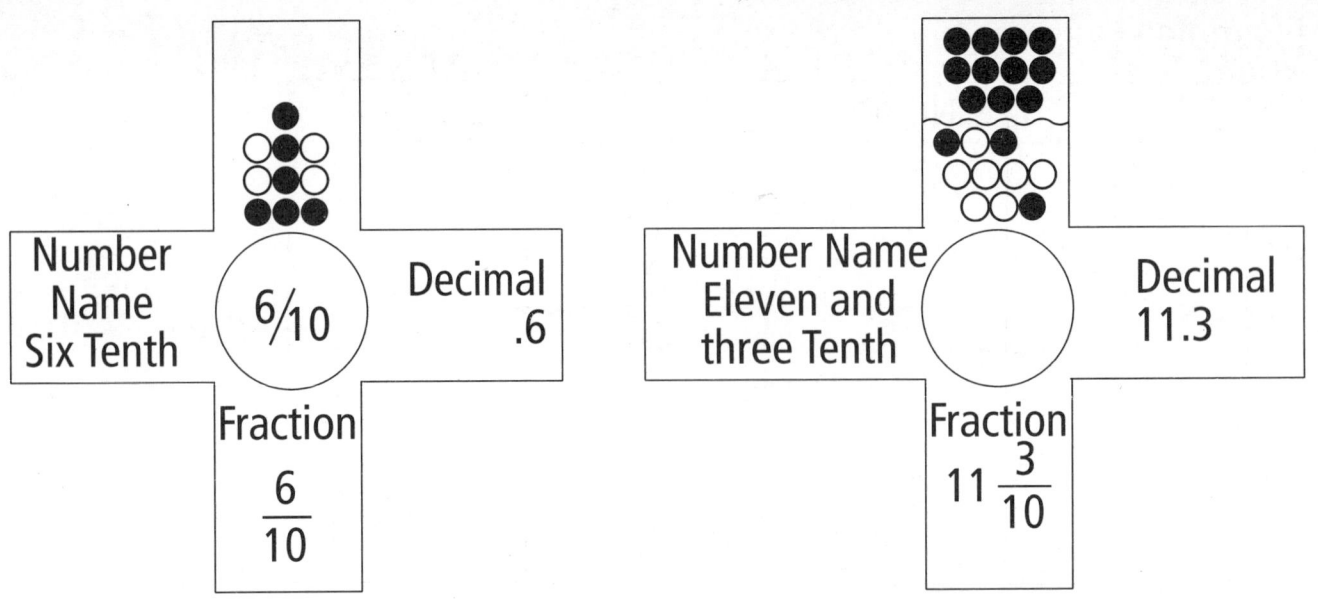

1. Write the number names for the following decimals.

a. 63.32 = Sixty three and thirty two hundreths.
b. 987.85 = _____
c. 8257.005 = _____
d. 73.650 = _____
e. 32.07 = _____

2. Write in the decimal form.

a. Two and four hundred seventy six thousandths = 2.476
b. Thirty five and seven hundreths = _____
c. Forty seven and six tenths = _____
d. Sixty and one hundreths = _____
e. Seventy five and two thirty one thousandths = _____

Remember: Adding zeroes to the right of a decimal number does not change its value.

So, we can easily convert the unlike decimals into like decimals without changing their values.

Example:-
a. 0.362 and 0.7
   0.361 and 0.700 [Like decimals]

b. 2.905 and 2.8
    2.905 and 2.800 [Like decimals]

1. Write decimal place to match the statements. The first one is done for you:

a. 9 in the ones place, 4 in the tens place, 6 in the the hundreths place and 0 in the tenths place. | 49.06 |

b. 7 in the tenths place, 6 in the tens place 4 in the hundredths place, 2 in the hundreds place and 0 in the ones place.
    | |

Decimal Power

Add:-
```
    3 1 . 0 0 1
    1 3 . 0 1 0
    1 3 1 . 0 0 0
  + 3 1 1 . 1 0 0
  _____
```

Even if we change the order of the addends, the sum remains the same. Any decimal number added to zero or zero added to any decimal no. gives the number itself.

Multiply:-
```
      3 . 4 8 5
    x 1 . 6 3
    _____
```

Subtract 16.28 from 36.486
First make the decimal numbers like then subtract putting the decimal pts. one below the other.

Subtract:-
```
      3 6 . 4 8 6
    - 1 6 . 2 8 0
    _____
```

Divide:-
18.24 by 8
```
    8 ) 1 8 . 2 4
```

Remember
To count the places after the decimal, put the decimal after those many places begining to count from the right. The decimal point will come directly above the decimal point in the dividend.

Solve the following word problems:-

1. A shopkeeper sold 35.5 kg apples, 25.25 kg mangoes and 15.15 kg of pears. What is the total weight of the fruits he sold that day?

   Qty. of Apples sold =

   _____ =

   _____ =

   Total weight = _____

   He sold _____ kg fruits that day.

2. Sum of three decimal numbers is 84.7. If two decimal numbers are 24.6 and 31.7, find the third number.

   First decimal number = _____

   Second decimal number = _____

   Sum = _____

   Sum of three decimal numbers = _____

   Sum of first two decimal numbers = _____

   Third decimal number = _____

3. If Emma requires 2.25 m cloth to stitch her skirt, how many skirts can be stitched with 20.25 m cloth?

   Total cloth = 20.25 m

   Cloth required for one skirt = 2.25 m

   Number of shirts that can be made 20.25 ÷ _____ = 2.25

5. Simplification of Numerical Expressions

Now we very well understand the four basic operations. When we need to carry out two or more operations at the same time, it is called a Numerical Expression.

To solve a numerical expression we need to follow

D	Division	1st
M	Multiplication	2nd
A	Addition	3rd
S	Subtraction	4th

DMAS Rule

Following DMAS:-

a. $18 + 4 \times 6 \div 2 - 9$

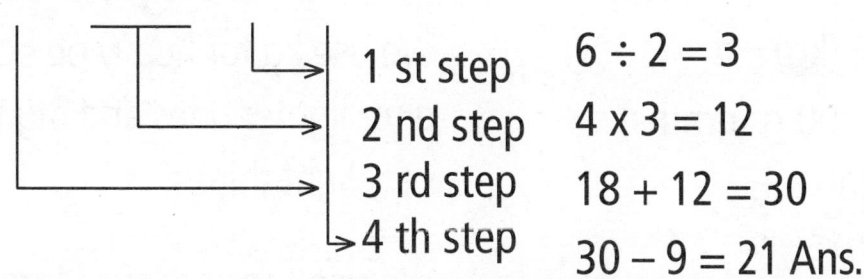

1 st step $6 \div 2 = 3$
2 nd step $4 \times 3 = 12$
3 rd step $18 + 12 = 30$
4 th step $30 - 9 = 21$ Ans.

Solve the following numerical expressions.

a. $\dfrac{1}{2} + \dfrac{3}{10} \div \dfrac{3}{5} =$ _____

b. $17 \times 3 + 81 \div 9 - 60 =$ _____

c. $3.6 \div 0.9 \times 0.5 - 2 =$ _____

d. $8 \div 8 \times 8 \div 8 - 8 + 8 =$ _____

Solve & compare the expressions.

a. $\dfrac{3}{5} \times \dfrac{2}{3} + \dfrac{7}{10} - \dfrac{1}{2} \bigcirc \dfrac{3}{5} + \dfrac{2}{3} \times \dfrac{7}{10} + \dfrac{1}{2}$

b. $16 - 5 \times 2 + 3 \bigcirc 16 - 5 + 3 \times 2$

c. $20 \div 4 \times 3 + 3 - 8 \bigcirc 15 \div 3 \times 4 + 5 - 15$

d. $15 + 6 - 5 \times 2 \bigcirc 3 \times 2 + 10 - 3$

6. Measurement (Length, Mass & Capacity)

Measurement
- Length
- Mass
- Capacity

Length   Kilometre (km)
1 km = 1000 m (metres)
1 m = 100 cm (centimetre)
1 cm = 100 mm (millimetre)

We use kms for longer distances and M and cm for shorter lengths and mm for extremely small things.

Mass   Kilogram (kg)
1 kg = 1000 g (grams)
1 g = 1000 mg

We use kg for heavy objects, g for lighter ones and mg for very light things.

Capacity   Litre
1 l = 1000 ml (milliletre)

We use l to measure larger quantity of liquids and ml for smaller quantity of liquids.

Common things which help to measure:

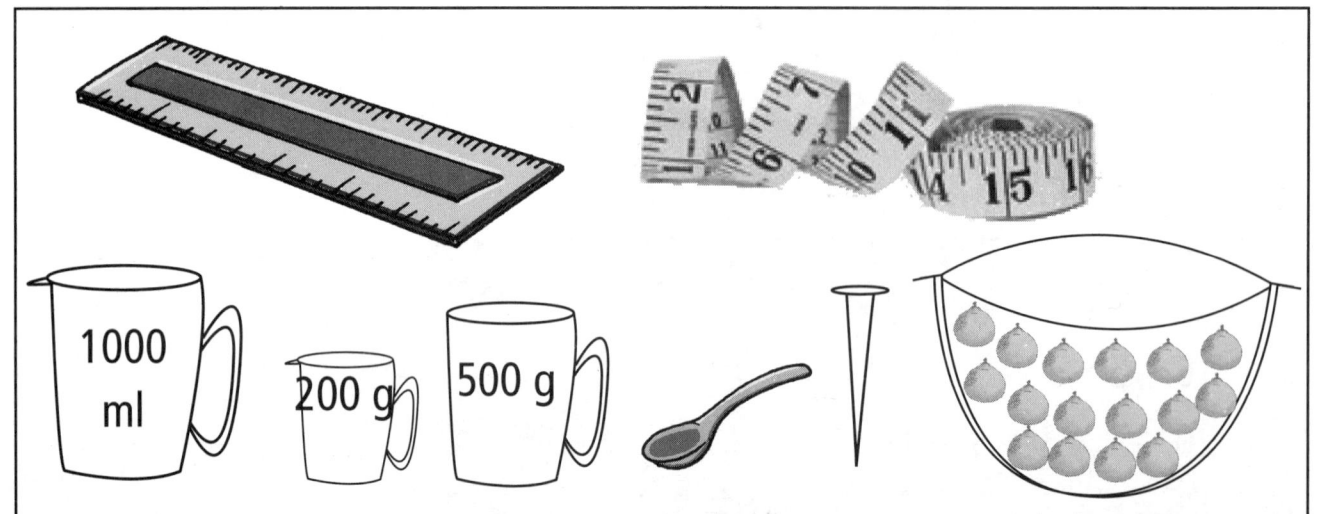

1. **Convert from one unit to another as mentioned below.**
   a. 1 km = _____ m.
   b. 2800 m = _____ km.
   c. 1250 m = _____ km _____ m.
   d. 5 km = _____ m.
   e. 1 kg = _____ g.
   f. 500 g = _____ kg
   g. 12.1 kg = _____ kg _____ g.
   h. 8008 g = _____ kg _____ g.
   i. 950 g = _____ kg.
   j. 1 l = _____ ml.
   k. 750 ml = _____ l.
   l. 4560 l = _____ l _____ ml.
   m. 2500 ml = _____ l _____ ml
   n. 3000 ml = _____ l.
   o. 1520 ml = _____ l.

2. **Guess true or false, tick the correct answer & put a cross for the wrong ones.**
   a. Herry is the tallest in class, having length 180 cm. _____
   b. Distance from Delhi to Mumbai is 200 km. _____
   c. Length of my pencil is 16 cm. _____
   d. My mother's shawl is 20 metre long. _____
   e. My study table is 2.5 m long. _____
   f. A new born baby is 3835 g. _____
   g. A box of cherries weighs 500 g. _____
   h. A cake weighs 3 kg. _____

3. **Circle the correct answer.**

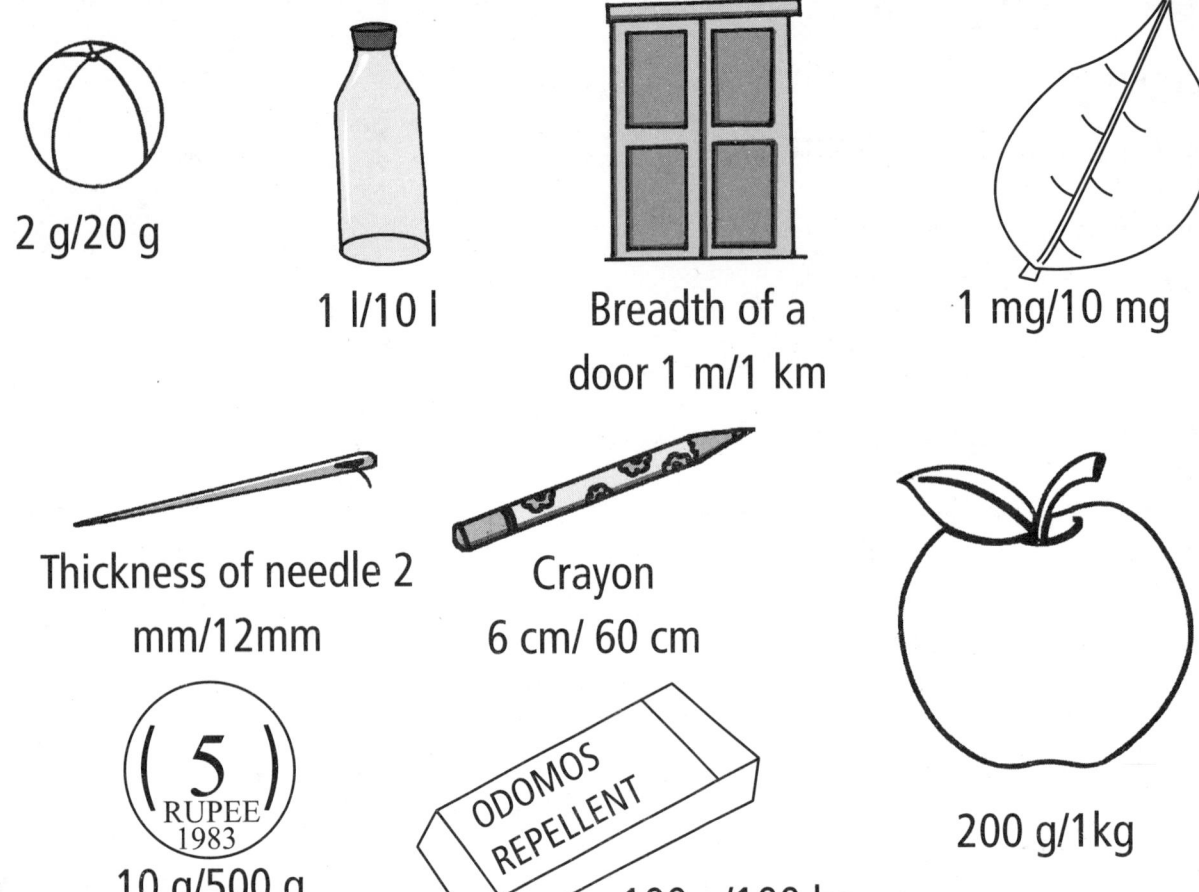

4. **Fill in the blanks with correct units.**

a. An aeroplane is about 900 _____ long.

b. A bottle of pepsi has around 250 _____ of pepsi.

c. The length of a tennis racket is about 1 _____ long.

d. A pair of shoes weigh around 1.5 _____.

e. Water in a fish aquarium is about 30 _____.

f. Thickness of a finger nail is about 1 _____.

g. The width of a pen is about 12 _____.

h. A grasshopper is about 6 _____ long.

i. A full suitcase weighs around 10 _____.

j. A bucket of water weighs around 20 _____.

7. Basic Shapes

Let's know about various solid shapes, their faces, corners & edges. Also write 1 example each for the given figures.

3 dimensional shape of solids.

Shapes	Faces	Corners	Edges	Example
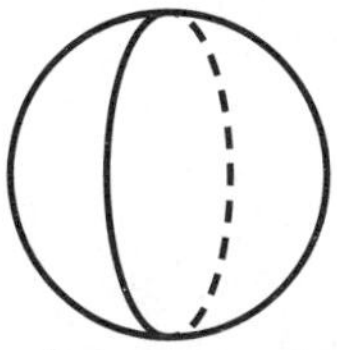 (Sphere)				Ball
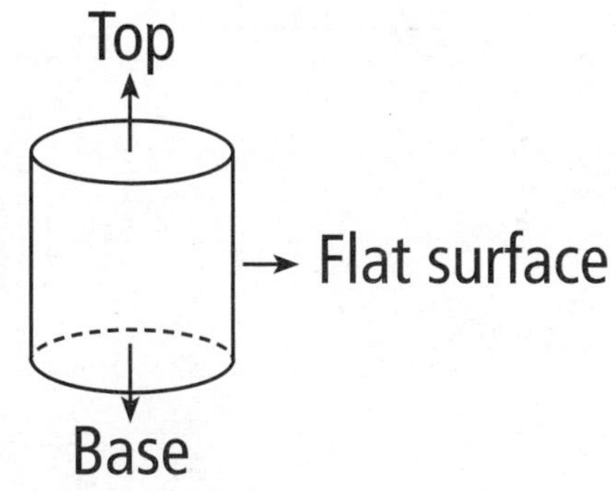 (Cylinder)				Gas cylinder
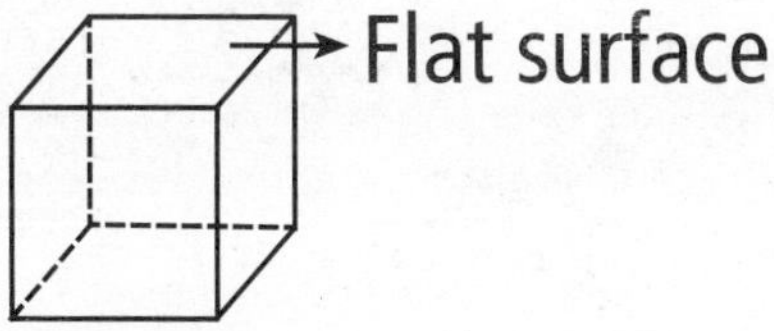 (Cube)				Dice
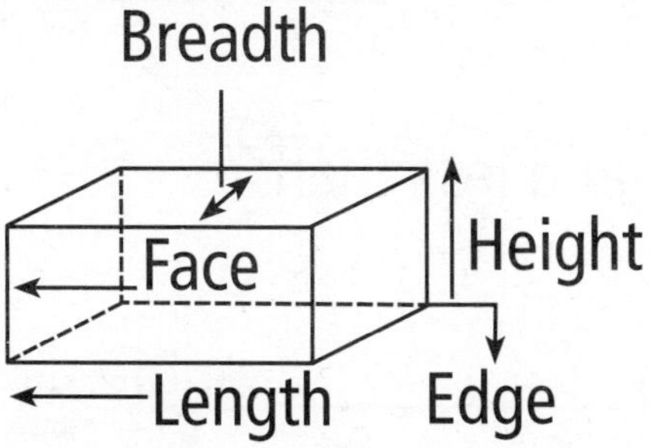 (Cuboid)				_____
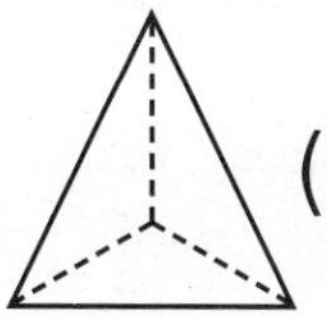 (Pyramid)	3	4	6	_____

2. Quickly name the shapes which are given below.

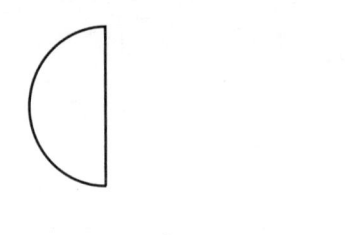 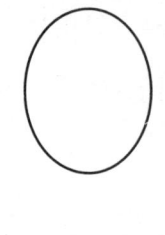 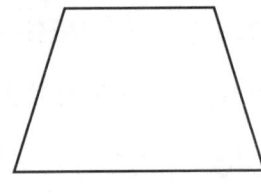

_____   _____   _____

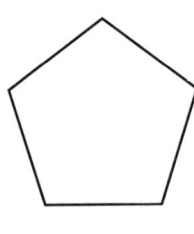 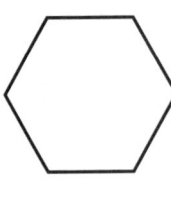 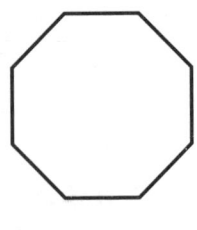

_____   _____   _____

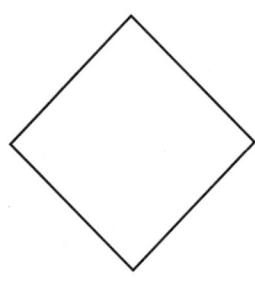 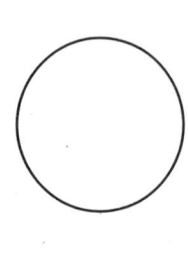

_____   _____

3. Fill in the blanks.

a. A part of a line that has two end points is a _____.

b. You cannot measure a ray as it keeps extending from _____ side.

c. An obtuse angle is more than _____° and less than _____°.

d. An angle which measures less than 90° is an _____ angle.

e. A right angle measures exactly _____°.

8. Angles and Triangles

Remember: If this angle is divided into 180 equal parts (shown below), then each part is called an angle of one degree which (degree) is the unit of measuring an angle. One degree is written as 1°.

Remember: A circle has 360°

Draw angles with the help of a protactor

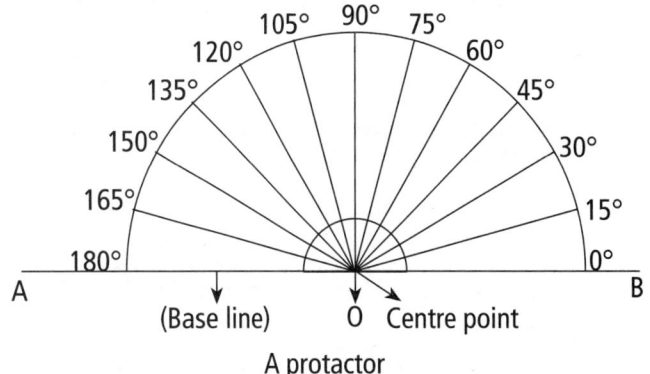

A protactor

a. ∠45°

b. ∠90°

c. ∠135°

d. ∠180°

e. ∠120°

Triangles

- Remember, a triangle has 3 vertices (corners), 3 sides & 3 angles.
- The sum of all the three angles of a △ is always 180°.
- The sum of any two sides of a △ is always greater than the third side.

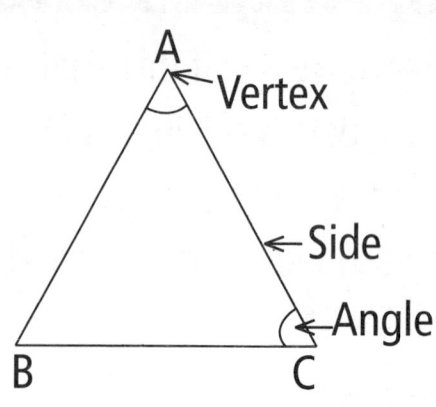

△ can be classified according to sides
- Scalene △ (different lengths)
- Isoceles △ (any two sides of same length)
- Equilateral △ (all three sides are equal)

According to angles
- Acute angled △ (whose all angles are acute)
- Obtuse angled △ (whose one angle is obtuse)
- Right angled △ (whose any one angle is a right angle)

1. Identify the following △s.

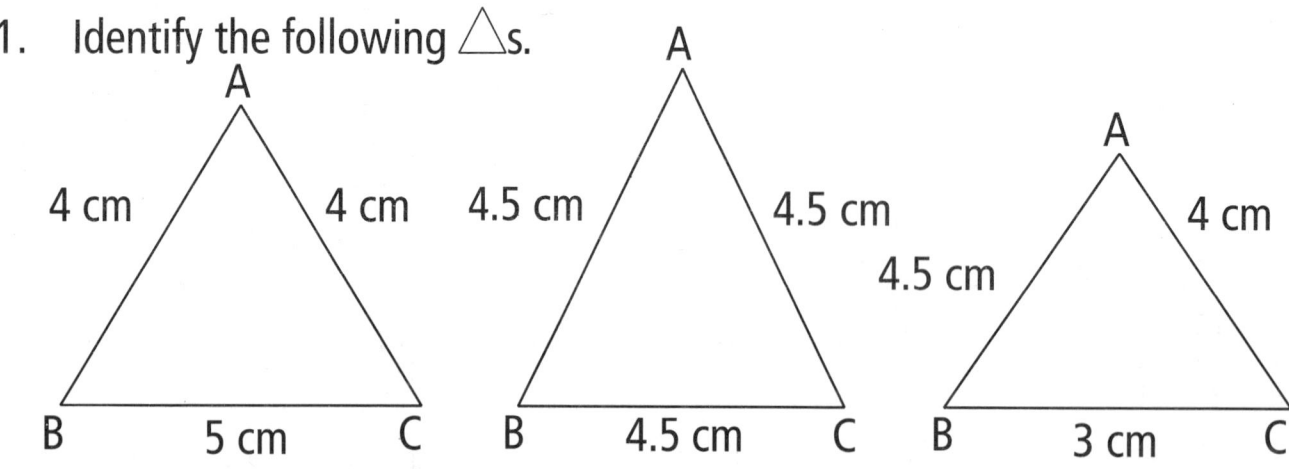

_____   _____   _____

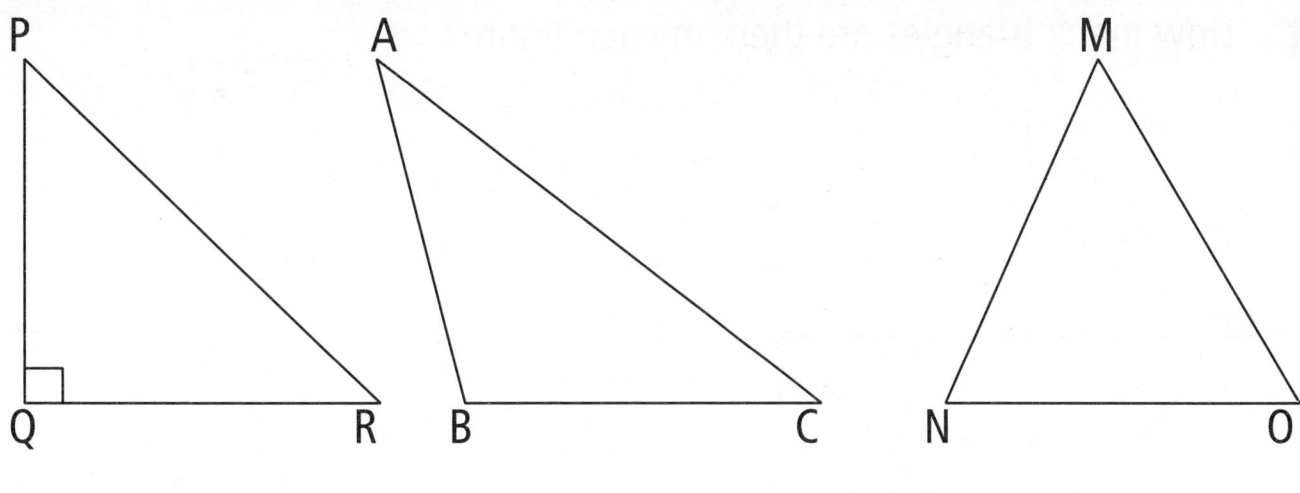

_____   _____   _____

2. Find the third ∠ in the given △.

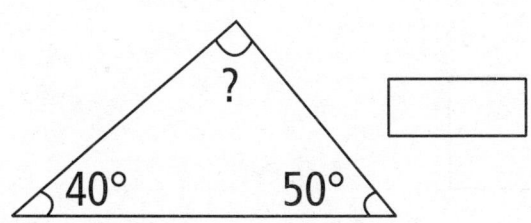   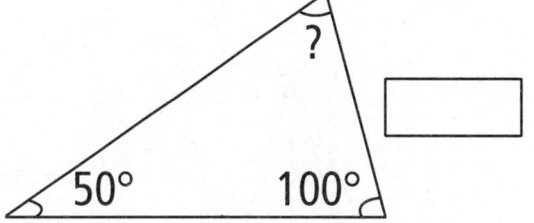

3. Fill in the blanks

a. If sum of two ∠s of a △ is 90°, the third angle of the △ will be _____.

b. If the measure of one angle of a right angled △ is 46°, find the other two ∠s _____, _____.

c. Can a △ have two obtuse angles? Yes/No

d. Can a △ have two right angles? Yes/No

e. Sum of lengths of any two sides of a △ is equal to the third side? Yes/No

f. A closed figure which is made of three line segments is called a _____.

4. How many triangles are there in each figure?

a.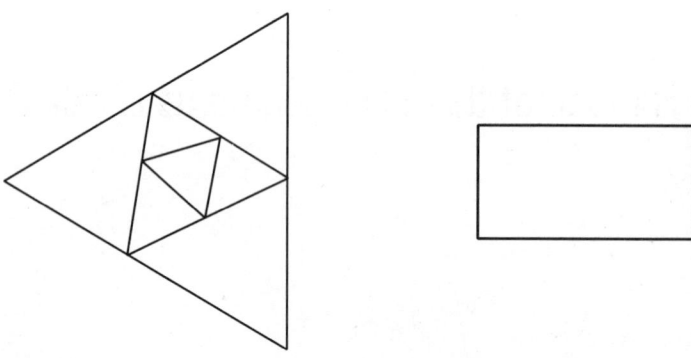

b.

c.

d.

9. Perimeter and Area

Perimeter is the distance around the edge of a figure while **Area** is the amount of surface that the figure covers.

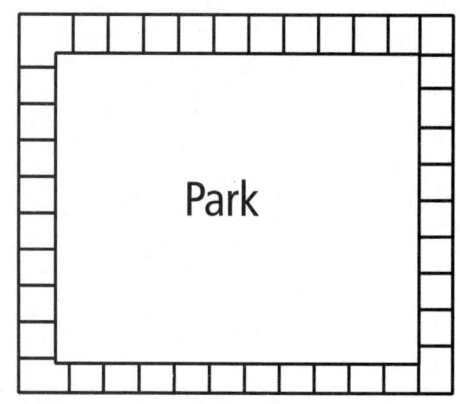

If the park has to be fenced it will be done as per the length of all the sides i.e. the Perimeter.

Perimeter = 4 x Side

Area of the park can be calculated by multiplying the length with its breadth. Area = L x B

Perimeter of different figures.

Perimeter of a triangle

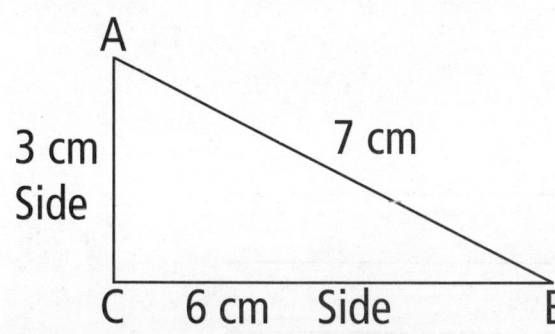

= AB + BC + CA
= (7 + 6 + 3)cm
= 16 cm

Note:- A triangle has 3 sides and 3 vertices.

Perimeter of a circle

The perimeter of a circle is the length of its circular boundary.

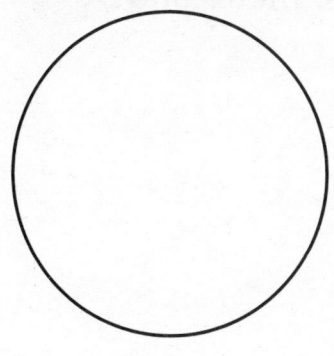

Note:-
A circle has neither side nor vertex.
Circumference:-
The circular boundary of a circle is called the circumference of the circle.

1. Study these plane figures and find their respective perimeter & area.

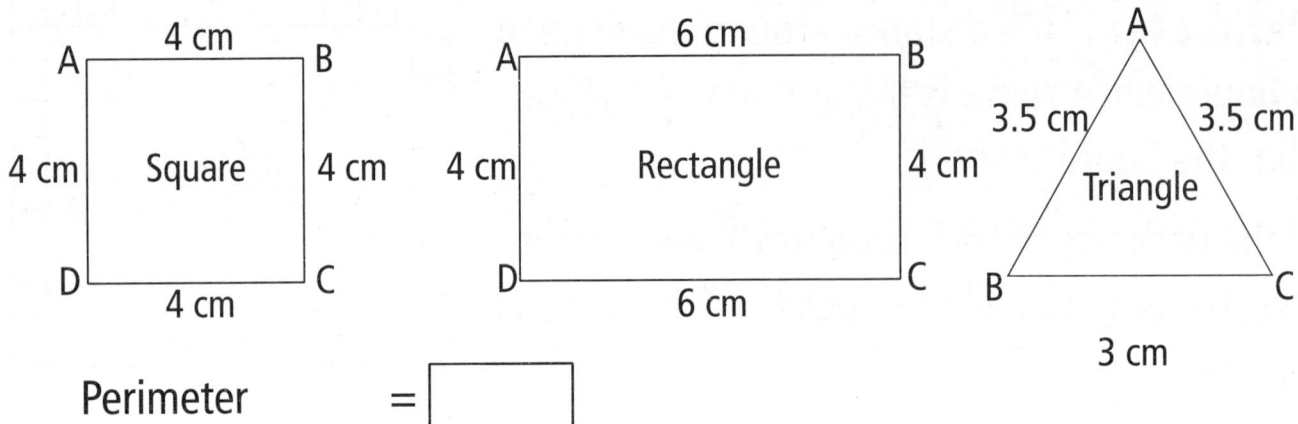

Perimeter = ☐

Area = ☐

Perimeter of square = 4 + 4 + 4 + 4 = 16 cm
Area of square = 4 x 4 = 16 sq. m
Area of a square and a rectangle
length x width
Area is represented in square metre.

Perimeter of rectangle = _____
Area of rectangle = _____
Perimeter of triangle = _____
Area of Triangle = _____

2. The length and the breadth of a swimming pool are 50 metre and 30 metre respectively. What will be its perimeter?

Perimeter of the swimming pool
= 2 length + 2 breadth
= 50 + 50 + 30 + 30 metre
= ☐ metre

Answer:
The perimeter of the swimming pool is ☐ metre.

3. Find the perimeter of a square-shaped room whose side is 15 metre.

   Perimeter of room = _____

4. A boy runs around a square field two times. Find the total distance covered by the boy if the length of the field is 250 metre. (Remember 1 kilometer = 1000 metres)

   Perimeter of the square shaped field

   = 4 x length of the field.

   = ☐ metre

   Boy ran two times around that field

   = 2 x perimeter

   = 2 x ☐ metre

   = ☐ kilometre.

   Answer: The boy covered total ☐ distance.

5. Fill in the columns to find the area:-

	Length	Breadth	Area
Washbasin wall	12 units	7 units	
Square painting	6 cm		
Carpet	7 m	5 m	
Mat	13 m		130 sq m

6. How many different rectangles can you make with an area of 24 sq cm? Find the perimeter of each one. See the example & follow. Also draw their respective figures.

a. Rectangle L x B = 24 x 1 sq cm.

   Perimeter 2 (L+B) = 50 cm.

b.

c.

d.

24 cm

1cm

10. Mathematics in Daily Life

Averages

There are several situations in our daily life where we need to find the average. Suppose weight of 15 children of a certain age group is taken. How can we know the average weight of that age group:-

$$\text{Average} = \frac{\text{Sum of addends}}{\text{Total number of addends}}$$

Weight of 20 students in the age group 8-10 yrs:-

24 kg, 25 kg, 18 kg, 19.5 kg, 17.5 kg, 21.5 kg, 20 kg, 27 kg, 20.5 kg, 22 kg, 26 kg, 19 kg, 18.5 kg, 25.5 kg, 17 kg

$$\text{Average weight} = \frac{(24 + 25 + 18 + 19.5 + 17.5\ 21.5 + 20 + 27 + 20.5 + 22 + 26 + 19 + 18.5 + 25.5 + 17)}{15}$$

$$= \frac{321}{15} = 21.5 \text{ kg}$$

Average weight of children of the age group 8 - 10 yrs is 21.5 kg.

Similarly we can do the following exercises.

Exercises:-

1. 5 parcels weigh 20 kg, 18 kg, 22 kg, 16 kg and 24 kg, find the average of the 5 parcels.

   = ☐ + ☐ + ☐ + ☐ + ☐ kg.

   $= \dfrac{\text{Weight of 5 parcels}}{\text{No. of Parcels}} = \dfrac{☐}{☐}$

   Answer: Average weight of 5 parcels is ☐ kg.

2. 4 friends shared the cost of a dinner. They spent an average of $ 25 each. What was the total cost of the Dinner.

    = Average cost x Number of friends

    = [ ] x [ ] = [ ]

    Answer: Total cost of dinner was [ ] dollars.

3. On an average Albert spends 4 hours studying every day during examination days. How much time does he spent in studying over 2 weeks? (1 week = 7 days)

    [ ] x [ ] = [ ]

4. 10 people gave donation and the total amount collected was 130. What was the average amount given by ten people?

    = $\frac{\square}{\square}$ dollars.

5. A shop keeper sold 10 televisions on Monday, 12 on Tuesday, 8 on Wednesday, 11 on Thursday, 6 on Friday and 13 on Saturday. Sunday the market was closed. What is the average number of televisions sold by the shopkeeper during that week?

    No. of Televisions sold during one week ⇨

    Monday to Saturday in 6 days   = 10 + 12 + 8 + 11 + 6 + 13

    = [ ] Televisions

    Average number of televisions sold by the shop keeper will be

    [ ] ÷ [ ] or $\frac{\square}{6}$

    Answer : Average number of televisions sold is [ ]

Application of Percentage: (Symbol %)

Cent means 100 (Percent means per hundred or out of 100)

Percent is a form of fraction with 100 as the constant denominator.

To convert a % in fraction we divide it by 100 and from a fraction to % we multiply by 100.

The fraction whose denominator is equal to hundred is called Percentage.

If Rohan gets 70 marks out of 100 he gets 70%. If Raman gets 40 out of 50 he gets 80%.

$$\frac{40}{50} \times 100 = 80\%.$$

If Seema takes 12 out of 20 pears she takes 60% of pears.

$$\frac{12}{20} \times 100 = 60\%$$

$$\frac{55}{100} = 55\% = 0.55 \text{ (in decimal form)}$$

$$\frac{11}{100} = \underline{}\% = 0.11 \text{ (in decimal form)}$$

$$\frac{33}{?} = 33\% = 0.33 \text{ (in decimal form)}$$

Example:-

Gauri has 10 pens in her pencil box, out of these 4 are blue, 3 are green, 2 are red and rest are black. Complete the following:-

Item	Number	Fraction	Decimal	%
Blue pens	4	4/10		40%
Red pens	2	2/10	0.2	
Green pens	3	3/10	0.3	
Black pens	1	1/10		10%

1. **Convert into lowest terms.**

   a. $6\frac{1}{4}\% = \frac{25}{4}\% = \frac{\cancel{25}}{4 \times \cancel{100}\,4} = \frac{1}{16}$

   b. $5.6\% = \frac{\cancel{56}\,28}{\cancel{10}\,5} = \frac{28}{5} = 5\frac{3}{5}$

   c. $7\frac{1}{7}\% =$

   d. $98\% =$

   e. $24\% =$

2. **Convert the following into percentages.**

   a. $\frac{6}{10} = \frac{6}{\cancel{10}} \times \cancel{100}\,10 = 60\%$

   b. $\frac{9}{50}$

   c. $1\frac{2}{5}$

   d. 9

   e. 0.01

   f. 0.045

3. **Find the following.**

   a. $33\% \text{ of } 1500 \text{ kg} = \frac{100}{3}\% \times 1500$

   $= \frac{\cancel{100}}{3 \times \cancel{100}} \times \cancel{1500}\,500 = 550 \text{ kg}$

   b. 30% of 60

   c. 150% of 20 litres

d. 20% of 5 kms.

4. **Compare the following. [Which is greater?]**

a. 8% of 200 gms or 10% of 100 gms.

b. 40% of 100 marks or 60% of 50 marks

5. **Find the percentage of the letter 'e' in the word 'percentage'.**

    [_____]

Simple Interest

Common terms (people dealing with bank)

Money deposited in bank **Principal**. Extra money paid by bank on the Principal amount **Simple Interest**. Period for which money is kept in bank **Time**. Money borrowed from the bank **Loan**. Extra money charged by the bank for every 100 rupees **Rate of Interest**.

Learn by heart

$$\text{Simple interest} = \frac{\text{Principal} \times \text{Rate of interest} \times \text{Time}}{100}$$

$$S.I = \frac{P \times R \times T}{100}$$

Complete the table.

S.No.	Principal	Rate of Interest	Time	S.I	Total Amt.
1.	$ 800	12%	2 yrs	$ 192	$ 992
2.	$ 12000	15%	4 yrs	$ 7200	$ 19200
3.	$ 2500	$4\frac{1}{2}$%	1 yr.		
4.	$ 3200	$6\frac{1}{2}$%	P.a.		
5.	$ 500	7%	$2\frac{1}{2}$ yrs.		

Principal	Simple Interest	Amount
a. $ 800	$ _____	$ 905
b. $ _____	$ 76.50	$ 1079.50
c. $ 20000	$ _____	$ 23575
d. $ _____	$ 157	$ 1530

1. Samantha deposited $ 5000 in a bank at 9% interest per annum. What will be the amount she got back after $2\frac{1}{2}$ years.

   _____

2. Samara took a loan of $ 3000 for $1\frac{1}{2}$ years with rate of interest of 7% p.a. Find the interest she pays after $1\frac{1}{2}$ yrs. Also calculate the amount she pays back after $1\frac{1}{2}$ years.

   _____

Temperature

An object or a body can be either hot or cold, to measure to check the degree of hotness or coldness of a body Temperature is used.

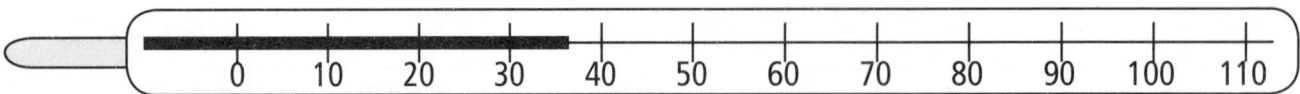

The instrument used to measure Temp = Thermometer

The unit used to measure Temp = degree

There are 2 scales —

    The Fahrenheit Scale [German Scientist]

    The Celsius Scale [Swedish Scientist]

Water

Freezing point	0°C	32°F
Boiling point	100°C	212°F

Normal Temp of a human body is 98.°6 F as shown on the clinical thermometer or 37°C.

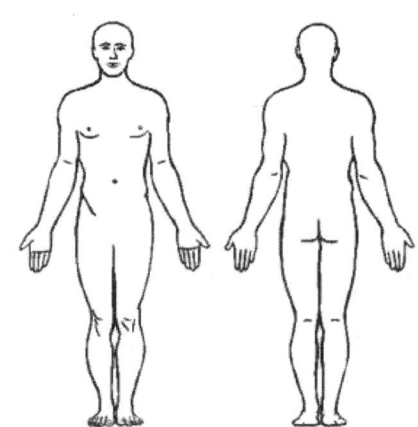

1. Convert in the Fahrenheit Scale

Conversion of Celsius Scale to the Fahrenheit Scale

Step 1. Multiply $\frac{9}{5}$ to the °C.

Step 2. Add 32 to the product.

    The result will be in °F.

Conversion of Fahrenheit Scale into Celsius Scale.

Step 1. Subtract 32 from given °F.

Step 1. Multiply remainder by $\frac{5}{9}$.

    Result will be in °C.

2. **Convert Fahrenheit Scale**
   a. 20°C

   $\dfrac{20}{4} \times \dfrac{9}{5} = 36 \Rightarrow 36 + 32 = 66°F$

   b. 75°C

   c. 100°C

3. **Convert into Celsius Scale**
   a. 95°F

   $95° - 32° = 63° \Rightarrow 63 \times \dfrac{5}{9} = 36 \Rightarrow 35°C$

   b. 212°F

   c. 110°F

Fill in the blanks

1. A doctor uses a _____ thermometer to measure the temperature of his patient.
2. The clinical thermometer has a _____ scale.
3. The temperature of a adult human body is _____ °F.
4. The two scales of a thermometer are _____ and _____.
5. _____ °C is the freezing point of water.
6. _____ °F is the boiling point of water.

11. Pictorial Representation of Data

1. In Modern school, London all the students of class X (section ABCD) have joined different hobbies.

Show the number of students according to the given list

Note: One (figure) is equal to 5 students of modern school, delhi, class X, section ABCD

HOBBIES		Interest in different hobbies							
Swimming	1	👤	👤	👤	👤	👤	👤	👤	
Drawing and Painting	2								
Music instrument	3								
Word craft	4								
Metal craft	5								
		5	10	15	20	25	30	35	40

Number of children

👤 = One figure represents 5 students

Number of students

Hobbies	–	No. of student
1. Swimming	–	30
2. Drawing and painting	–	25
3. Music instruments	–	20
4. Word craft	–	15
5. Metal craft	–	15

Place Los Angeles (Weather Record)

(Month: August, 2010)

Date Aug.	Days	Weather condition Sun Clouds Rain	Temperature maximum (12:30 pm) Temp. Centigrade	Temperature minimum (2:30 am) Temp. Centigrade
1	Monday	Sun	35.5	23.2
2	Tuesday	Sun	35.9	24.8
3	Wednesday	Sun with Clouds	35.2	22.6
4	Thursday	Clouds	34.8	22.8
5	Friday	Clouds	30.7	23.5
6	Saturday	Rain	28.9	22.2
7	Sunday	Rain	27.2	20.4

2 a. In August which day was pleasant having minimum day temperature

= _____ Day - Date _____ August

b. On which day in August temperature was maximum during day time

= _____

Do it yourself:-

Take the newspapers of last week, check the maximum and minimum temperature of the last ten days and write according to the above example.

The bar graph below shows the number of tourists who visited the Tower Bridge of London from Monday to Saturday.

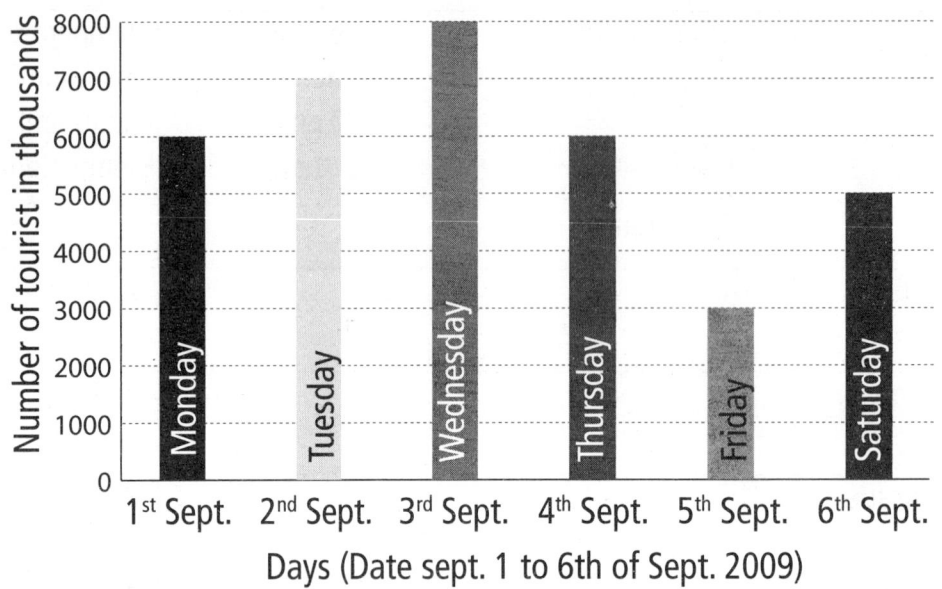

3 a. How many tourists visited the Tower Bridge of London on 6th of September, Saturday 2009. _____ _____.

b. On which day the number of tourists was minimum? ☐.

c. Which two days had the same number of tourists. On ☐ Day and ☐ Day dated ☐ and ☐, the number of tourists remained same ☐.

d. On which day the number of tourists was maximum? ☐

e. How many visitors were there in total on the 6 days from 1st September to 6th of September. 2009.

There were total ☐ tourists who visited the Tower Bridge of London during the 1st week of September 2009.